Diving with Nitrox
Theory for Scuba Divers

- A related to practice textbook -

Nitrox 1

incl. Questions and Answers

1. Edition

Diving with Nitrox

Author Karsten Reimer

Bibliographic Information of the German National library:

The German National library listed this publication in the German in the German National bibliography; detailed bibliographic data are available on the internet via http://dnb.dnb.de

1. Edition (English) March 2023

Karsten Reimer

Author

Production and publishing:

BoD – Books on Demand, Norderstedt, Germany

ISBN 9783749455614

All information contained in this book has been compiled to the best of my knowledge and based on decades of experience in the training of scuba divers and instructors. But since I am just a human, of course, mistakes could be possible, although I have had this book proofread by many other professionals. Thus, I can at least shift some of the blame to others, if this book should nevertheless contain mistakes. I am very sure that this book contains no serious mistakes and thus cannot provoke diving accidents. Nevertheless, I decline any liability, obligation or guarantee, should it come to an accident due to reading my book or due to any inaccuracy in this book. Therefore, I strongly recommend that you use this book only as a companion and as part of a professional dive training course by a professional instructor certified by a recognized association **(CMAS or R.S.T.C.)**. Even though there are no legal requirements for recreational divers in some countries, you should not go underwater with the SCUBA equipment without professional help. Protected trade names or trademarks or logos are not always specially marked. From the lack of such evidence cannot be concluded that it is a free brand name, a free trademark or a free company logo. Make sure before you commit a trademark infringement, because that could be very expensive for you. Not all companies accept this without complaint.

Foreword

This book is a guide to gaining the theoretical knowledge necessary to pass the exam for the dive course Nitrox 1. In this book, the male salutation is used to simplify the writing. Of course that does not mean that only men should dive. There are even voices in the "diving scene" claiming that women are the better divers. In view of the often irresponsible willingness to take risks of my male contemporaries, this is a thesis that I would definitely subscribe to.

Even though ☺

Divers are men who can live and work under water or in non-respirable air.
Divers are men of great muscle power, with healthy organs. There is no second profession that places as high demands on physical performance as the profession of the diver requires, not just occasionally. Wearing the almost 100 kg heavy armor outside the water, or the movement of this mass while walking under water, breathing under rapidly changing pressure and, not least, most strenuous work under not always perfect air supply, require athletic muscles, healthy lungs, strong heart and proper functioning of all organs. Divers are men of high spiritual powers, of intellect and impeccable morality. They have to defy such diverse dangers that the highest demands are placed on their presence of mind and observation. To do useful and fast diving work is at the same time the actual art of the diver, which makes his activity valuable. An unflinching sense of duty must drive him to provide the fastest and most effective solution to the task by giving all the powers of his body and mind.

Manual for divers
Hermann Stelzner
Director and Chief engineer of the Drägerwerk
*Lübeck **1931***

It may have been like that in 1931. Today, diving is possible for anyone. However, health is still an important requirement.

Content

Diving with Nitrox

Diving with Nitrox

If we take it exactly, we always use Nitrox, namely Nitrox 21. Since the number after the word Nitrox indicates the percentage of oxygen in the gas mixture. Nitrox is an artificial word made up of the two main gases that are used.

Nitrogen and **Ox**ygen

Abroad, one usually uses the term EAN or EANx, which stands for Enriched Air Nitrox.

Why should we, if possible, dive with Nitrox?

Diving with Nitrox has enjoyed increasing popularity for over 20 years and is one of the most booked courses worldwide. By using Nitrox as a breathing gas you can extend your dives or you can dive safer within the same dive time as with normal air with regard to nitrogen saturation. Even with several dives a day, so-called repetitive dives, there is a positive effect on health when diving with Nitrox. This effect is due to the fact that when we dive with nitrox, we take in less nitrogen. The normal breathing air with which we usually dive contains about 78% nitrogen and 21% oxygen. Both gases behave differently, depending on the ambient pressure, and thus their effect on the human body changes, depending on the pressure we are exposed to. The residual gases (1%) (noble gases, carbon dioxide, water vapor, etc.) are negligible.

The lower the nitrogen partial pressure, i.e. the proportion of nitrogen in the total gas mixture, the less is the risk of decompression sickness and the danger of a depth intoxication. In which, according to the latest research, the previously assumed reduced risk of getting a depth intoxication, seems to be like diving with air. Since oxygen, inhaled under increased pressure, has a narcotic effect too and thus differs only slightly from the nitrogen narcosis (depth intoxication). But this effect is currently only of a theoretical nature, because there are no empirical studies yet.

On the other hand, however, the proportion of oxygen in our gas mixture determines the maximum depth we are allowed to go to. The higher the oxygen content, the lower the allowed depth with the corresponding mixture. If you have internalized this theory lesson and successfully completed the course Nitrox with your instructor, you may dive with a maximum oxygen content of 40% in the mixture used.

If you then enjoy diving with different gases, you can visit many different courses offered by our IDA Instructors.

IDA Nitrox Advanced

Gas Blender (mix gases by yourself)

SCR (Semi-closed Rebreather)

Trimix* and ** (Nitrogen, Helium and Oxygen)

Nitrox-Basic-Instructor

Nitrox-Instructor

Nitrox-Instructor Examiner

Trimix-Instructor

Trimix-Instructor Examiner

But let's start very slowly.

When we start to dive with a different gas than normal breathing air, new terms come to mind that are due to the different compositions of Nitrox.

On this page we summarized and explained these.

EAN   Enriched Air Nitrox   = with oxygen enriched air

EANx   Enriched Air Nitrox   = with oxygen enriched air

MOD   Maximum Operating Depth   = Maximum depth of dive

MOP   Maximum Operating Pressure   = Maximum ambient pressure at the chosen depth

EAD   Equivalent Air Depth = Equivalent depth when diving with air

EAP   Equivalent Air Pressure   = Equivalent pressure when diving with air

Best Mix   =   Optimum mix for this depth and dive time

OTU   Oxygen Tolerance Unit   = Tolerated oxygen units

CNS   Central Nervous System   = Central Nervous System :-)

CNS O_2%   =   Relative toxicity of O2 for the CNS

NOAA   National Oceanic and Atmospheric Administration (USA)

Here are some examples of common nitrox compositions:

Nitrox 32 = 32% O_2 + 68% N_2 = **EAN 32**

Nitrox 36 = 36% O_2 + 64% N_2 = **EAN 36**

Nitrox 40 = 40% O_2 + 60% N_2 = **EAN 40**

IDA recommends a maximum oxygen partial pressure (ppO2) of 1.4 bar (pp stands for partial pressure)

Therefore, the oxygen content in the gas mixture automatically results in the maximum diving depth.

32 % is equal to 0,32 bar ppO_2 at the surface.

36 % is equal to 0,36 bar ppO_2 at the surface.

40 % is equal to 0,40 bar ppO_2 at the surface.

Based on a maximum oxygen partial pressure (gas partial pressure) of 1.4 bar, we come to the following water depths. We divide the 1.4 bar ppO2 by the oxygen partial pressure at the water surface and then receive the max. partial pressure of oxygen and can deduce the maximum depth of it.

Nitrox 32 (NOAA Nitrox 1) = 4,38 bar corresponds to 33,8 meter

Nitrox 36 (NOAA Nitrox 2) = 3,9 bar corresponds to 29 meter

Nitrox 40 = 3,5 bar corresponds to 25 meter

Nitrox 50 (Safe air) = 2,8 bar corresponds to 18 meter

 Attention, not always stands the oxygen content of the gas mixture at the first place. It is always necessary to analyze the mixture before use.

 In addition, other organizations have others standard gas mixtures.

So you have to check the oxygen content of the used mixture before <u>each</u> dive! Make sure your scuba tank is not swapped after oxygen analysis.

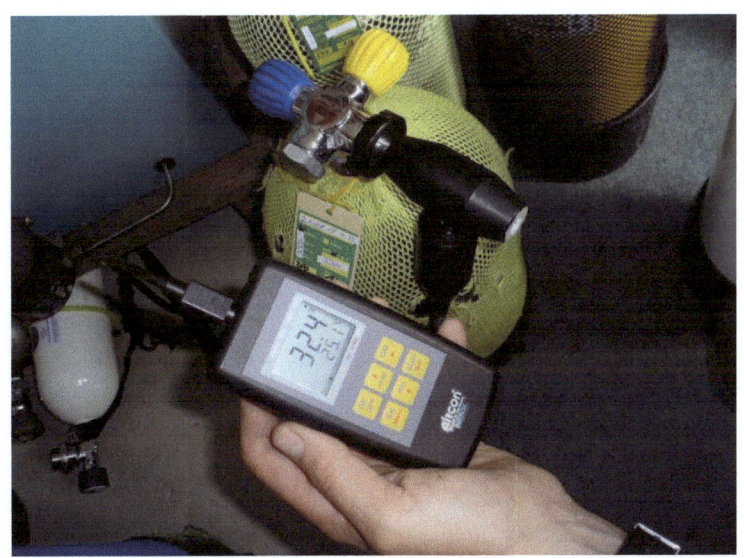

The previous analysis shows an oxygen content of 32.4%!

So Nitrox 32!

The gas mixture should always be mixed as precisely as possible and the difference to the calculated gas, should always be as low as possible, but at any rate below 1%, larger differences can lead to accidents or even death. Get yourself introduced to the analyzer if you do not have an own with whom you have gained experience. Always check the oxygen content of your breathing air yourself!

What is oxygen?

Oxygen (O_2)

- is a colorless and odorless element

- is a molecule in double bond

- boiling point: -183° C

- density: 1,429 Kg/m^3

- is not flammable in pure form

- is necessary for the combustion process

- acts as an oxidizer

- acts as a fire accelerator with increasing

  Concentration

What is nitrogen?

Nitrogen (N_2)

- is a colorless and odorless element

- is a molecule in double bond

- boiling point: -194,6° C

- density: 1,25 Kg/m^3

- makes as "inert gas" hardly any biochemical connection

What is carbon dioxide?

Carbon dioxide (CO_2)

- is a compound of 1 atom C and 2 atoms O_2

- is colorless and odorless

- is easily soluble in liquids (e. g. in mineral water)

- boiling point: -78,5° C

- density: 1,977 Kg/m^3

Gases and their application limits!

Oxygen

Minimal ppO_2 = 0,16 bar

Maximum ppO_2 = 1,4 bar

Nitrogen

At approx. 3.2 bar ppN2, an increased anesthetic symptom (depth intoxication) can be expected.

Carbon dioxide

Maximum ppCO2 0.05 bar in the arterial blood (from 0.06 bar ppCO2 hypercapnia can be expected and CO2 anesthesia can occur)

The partial pressures in the water depth can be easily calculated by multiplying the partial pressure of the individual gas at the water surface, with the ambient pressure in the depth.

Example

32 % oxygen is equal to a partial pressure (ppO_2) of 0,32 bar

In 20 meters of water, there is an ambient pressure of 3.0 bar.

So we now multiply the ambient pressure with the partial pressure and thus come to the partial pressure, which prevails at this specific depth.

0,32 bar ppO_2 x 3,0 bar = 0.96 bar ppO_2

Our oxygen partial pressure at a water depth of 20 meters is therefore 0.96 bar. So completely uncritical.

We know that we are allowed to have a maximum oxygen partial gas pressure of 1.4 bar. So we can divide 1.4 bar by 0.32 bar to come to the maximum allowable ambient pressure.

1.4 bar divided by 0.32 bar gives 4.375 bar

This 4.375 bar is the maximum permissible ambient pressure with an oxygen content of 32%.

We have 4.375 bar ambient pressure in a water depth of 33.75 meters. (We have to subtract the 1.0 bar air pressure at the surface, i.e. 3.375 bar water pressure)

This results in a maximum permitted depth of 33.75 meters with an oxygen content of 32%!

This calculation can be used for any gas mixture.

If you want, you can also use the following formula.

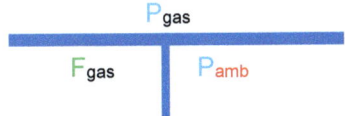

P_{Gas} stands for the partial pressure of the gas.

F_{Gas} stands for the percentage of the gas.

P_{amb} stands for the ambient pressure.

F stands for fraction (proportion).

amb stands for ambient (surroundings)

P stands for pressure.

This formula is a help to obtain the single pressures. It states that you must either multiply or divide each factor to arrive at the value you are looking for.

Partial pressure: F_{gas} multiplicated with P_{amb} is P_{gas}

Ambient pressure: P_{gas} divided by F_{gas} is P_{amb}

Gas proportion: P_{gas} divided by P_{amb} is F_{gas}

If you now hide the number you are looking for, the calculation with the open numbers (times or divide) shows the result. Of course, you only have to use this procedure if you want to mix your own gases and go diving with them. If you dive with Nitrox at any dive center in the world, it is important to analyze the content of your own scuba tank before the dive. And if the oxygen content is not right, get another scuba tank. But then check the oxygen content again, please.

Now a few sample calculations for understanding.

1. The maximum oxygen partial pressure should be 1.4 bar. The mixture has a 28% oxygen content. What maximum ambient pressure is allowed?

We are looking for P_{amb}

Ambient pressure: P_{gas} divided by F_{gas} is P_{amb}

$$\frac{1{,}4 \text{ bar}}{0{,}28} = 5 \text{ bar}$$

5 bar prevail in a water depth of 40 meters!

2. Same values but now we are looking for the oxygen content.

Gas proportion: P_{gas} divided by P_{amb} is F_{gas}

$$\frac{1{,}4 \text{ bar}}{5 \text{ bar}} = 0{,}28 \text{ is 28\% oxygen proportion.}$$

3. Again the same values but now we want to calculate the partial pressure.

Partial pressure: F_{gas} times P_{amb} is P_{gas}

0,28 x 5 bar = 1,4 bar

And now you can, if you like, calculate all the necessary values.

MOD

stands for Maximum Operating Depth and indicates the maximum permitted depth with a specific mixture.

In order to calculate the MOD, we first need the

MOP

MOP stands for Maximum Operating Pressure and indicates the maximum permitted ambient pressure.

We calculate a test dive with 36% oxygen content.

Maximum oxygen partial pressure may be 1.4 bar, which we have now internalized.

36% oxygen content is also given.

$$\frac{1{,}4 \text{ bar}}{0{,}36} = 3{,}89 \text{ bar}$$

Thus 3,89 bar is the **MOP**

Since we know that we always have to subtract 1 bar surface pressure to get to the pure water pressure, we now subtract 1 bar from the 3.89 bar and thus get 2.89 bar.

We have 2.89 bar water pressure at a depth of 28.9 meters. Thus, 28.9 meters is our MOD. We should not dive deeper with this mixture.

We make sure by looking at page 4 and find everything fits. Correctly calculated.

And now just stick to the depth specifications on page 153 and stay within no-stop times, then you're on the safe side. And even if you have to make a decompression stop, you're still on the safe side when diving with Nitrox. Since you have less nitrogen in your breathing gas mixture but still decompress according to a table (e. g. Deko 2000), which assumes a higher nitrogen content.

Advantage of Nitrox

Theoretically, you could, if you have practiced the calculations, extend the no-stop times in a specific depth (keyword EAD). But that makes little sense in normal diving on holiday, because then you increase the risk of a decompression accident and lose the advantage of Nitrox. Namely the greater security against a decompression accident.

The same applies to the decompression times, which you could theoretically shorten if you perform the corresponding calculations.

The reduced nitrogen content of your breathing air reduces the risk of microbubble formation. Microbubbles, as the name implies, are microscopic gas bubbles that actually form on each dive, but do not cause damage if we stay within the no-stop time or decompress properly.

Due to the lower nitrogen content of the breathing air, of course, the burden on the body by the nitrogen is lower. Thus, the risk of a depth intoxication is, at least theoretically, reduced and also the risk of suffering a decompression accident.

In addition, there are divers who feel fresher and less exhausted after diving with Nitrox. Often only after the second dive.

For divers which make several dives a day, instructor assistants, dive guides and instructors, Nitrox is the mixture of choice.

Disadvantage of Nitrox

What has advantages, experience has shown, has unfortunately also disadvantages. Of course this also applies to Nitrox.

- Due to the increased oxygen content, the burden on the central nervous system of humans is also higher. However, if you strictly adhere to the depth limits and do not exceed them, nothing can happen to you. But it must not be concealed that there are people who nevertheless get problems with the increased oxygen content.

This is very seldom and you can also get used to the increased oxygen content. Just as Reinhold Meßmer got used to climbing Mount Everest without oxygen. However, if you feel unwell when diving with Nitrox, leave the water and dive furthermore with air. If you want to get to the root of the problem, you can go to a specialist and undergo an oxygen tolerance test. Unfortunately, the health insurance does not pay this test. But as I said, this happens only very rarely.

- With Nitrox you should not dive as deep as with normal air.

- The equipment, especially the valves and the regulators, must be "oxygen clean", meaning that special seals must be used and no grease must be used. Oxygen and grease (silicone grease etc.) are natural enemies and when they come together it can get pretty loud.

- Oxygen promotes combustion (oxidation).

- The filling station must be specially designed.

- The filling costs are increased, at least for the base operator.

- The dive must be planned and calculated very carefully. The MOD must be adhered to. Even though my often quoted golden treasure is lying beneath you, under no circumstances should you dive deeper than the MOD allows.

- With your special nitrox tank, you must not go to a "normal" air filling station, as you get there no absolutely grease and oil-free air. Even if the amount of oil in the air mixture is extremely low, these small proportions may accumulate over time and explode when they get in touch with pure oxygen.

- It must / should always be dived with a Nitrox suitable diving computer and the maximum oxygen partial pressure (1.4 bar) and the mixture used (EAN 32 or EAN 36) must always be entered and checked prior to the dive.

- Some countries in the EU require a special regulator thread (M26 x 2).

- The utensils used (regulator, diving equipment, inflators) must be checked and cleaned once a year to detect and eliminate any accumulation of grease or oil.

- Generally you can go diving with nitrox in mountain lakes (Altitude Diving, i.e. at altitudes ≥ 300 meters) too. However, as there are no validated data available, you should dive as if you were using normal air (21% oxygen).

The US National Oceanic and Atmospheric Administration (NOAA) states that we can use our normal equipment, with no modification, up to 40% oxygen in the breathing gas mixture. This directive has been used in the United States for many years and has proven itself. In Europe, however, there are also other opinions. In Germany, for example, any gas mixture which has more than 21% oxygen content, is to treat as pure oxygen. However, it should not be concealed that during the filling and mixing process, when filling by partial pressure method, explosions are possible if oils and / or grease that are not oxygen-compatible are located on or in the scuba tank. The partial pressure filling method uses pure oxygen (100%). Therefore, only oxygen-clean diving tanks may be filled according to this method.

Medical aspects of diving with Nitrox

What happens if we exceed the MOD (Maximum Operating Depth) when using a specific gas mixture?

When we exceed this depth limit, a **hyperoxia** occurs. Hyper means too much and Oxie stands for oxygen. This simply means too much oxygen. In this case, too much oxygen pressure. As already mentioned, we should avoid an oxygen partial pressure of over 1.4 bar. But, as is sometimes the case, the risk attracts us and we want to see where our limits are. That is completely human and therefore often stupid.

Paul Bert found out as early as 1878 that oxygen, inhaled under increased pressure, has a toxic effect on the body. This increased oxygen partial pressure has a narcotic effect on the central nervous system (CNS). This effect is named in honor of Mr. Bert also Paul-Bert effect.

What exactly happens to us when we inhale the oxygen with a partial pressure of more than 1.4 bar?

At the same time, two things happen to our body.

Symptom No. 1

Central nervous system (CNS) disorders, Paul-Bert effect

Neurotoxic effects of hyperoxia

- Muscle tremors, twitching and cramps

- Eye disorders, blurred vision

- Malaise, nausea

- Hallucinations, confusion, metallic taste

- Inner ear disorders, ear noises

If you notice it by yourself, it is necessary to ascend several meters immediately. It is best to leave the water after the safety stop (3 minutes at 5 meters) has been carried out. Conclusion: Be sure to always and especially when using Nitrox, **never exceed** the 1.4 bar oxygen partial pressure.

The general oxygen tolerance limit in humans is an oxygen partial pressure of 1.82 bar and an exposure time of one minute. For us recreational divers that is less important but the colleague who operates the pressure chamber, if we have miscalculated, should know that. Pressure chamber treatments typically begin with 100% oxygen at 18 meters of simulated water depth. The patient is lying and gets 20 minutes of pure oxygen and then follows a 5 minute oxygen break. The problem with the seizures is tolerated, because usually the patient has bigger problems than a seizure in a controlled environment. (Note from the pressure chamber operator).

Symptom No. 2

The lung effect, also called Lorraine-Smith effect.

Oxygen is a very reactive gas and has the property to damage the alveoli under increased pressure and long exposure time. Symptoms of this oxygen overpressure are:

- Damage to the lung tissue (alveoli)

- Irritation of the pharyngeal mucosa

- Burning and stinging in the eyes

- Unstoppable cough

- Possibly unconsciousness

- Hypoxia (lack of oxygen) due to damage to the alveoli

In the worst case, the increased oxygen partial pressure can cause bursting of the alveoli. This reduces the lung surface, which is essential for gas exchange, resulting in reduced oxygen uptake and reduced carbon dioxide release. Ignoring this "ability" of oxygen, it can come to the point where the effective lung surface is so greatly reduced that the affected person suffocates.

And if you now believe that you can dive indefinitely as long as you don't exceed the 1.4 bar oxygen partial pressure, you are unfortunately wrong. At least from a medical point of view. But the time you can stay under this pressure without taking damage is 153 minutes, and before that happens you are freezing or thirsty. Keyword OTU.

What means OTU?

The oxygen tolerance unit, abbreviated OTU, is a value indicating the permissible oxygen units.

A unit is composed of the amount (partial pressure) of the oxygen in the breathing gas mixture and the pressure (ambient pressure) at which we inhale this mixture. Both values add up to the OTU and show us, according to the table, how many units we can consume safely.

For example, you can breathe in a breathing gas mixture with a low oxygen content and at a low ambient pressure over a long period of time without being harmed. You can already tell by the fact that we can breathe in the 21% oxygen contained in our normal breathing air for a very long time, a whole life long, without suffering excessive damage.

But if we now increase the amount of oxygen in our breathing air, let's say to 50%, then the time we can breathe in that mixture without suffering any damage is considerably shorter. If we now increase the proportion of oxygen to 100% and breathe in this gas under normal pressure, it comes and there are the physicians seemingly not really agree, after several days to a damage of the body.

If we now increase the pressure, we multiply the damaging potential of oxygen by compressing it. For example by diving to a certain depth, the time that we can inhale this breathing gas safely reduces to a few hours or even minutes.

Note: The higher the proportion of oxygen in the breathing gas mixture and the higher the pressure at which we inhale this mixture, the more damaging this gas is to our body.

In the following table you can see which oxygen partial pressure (PO2 or ppO2) you can breathe safely and how long you can. IDA recommends always staying under 700 units (OTU) per day.

We will come to the CNS later, but again only 80% of the allowed oxygen uptake should be used to avoid damage. Now, if you go on a longer dive holiday and dive with Nitrox daily, you must remember that the harmful effects of oxygen breathed under increased pressure **add up**. For this reason, the daily tolerable OTU value is reduced every day. From the 7th day you should absolutely take one day diving break. In addition, you should have at least one hour of surface break between each dive a day. If you are still allowed to consume 700 OTUs on the first day, the maximum tolerable OTU value for the following days is reduced as follows:

2. Day 620 OTU

3. Day 525 OTU

4. Day 460 OTU

5. Day 420 OTU

6. Day 380 OTU

7. Day 300 OTU

Diving break

(do something nice with the family) :-)

PO$_2$ (bar)	OTU (1/min.)	CNS (%/min.)	Dive Time max. (min.)
0,50	0,00	0,00	>
0,60	0,26	0,14	714
0,64	0,35	0,15	666
0,66	0,39	0,16	625
0,68	0,43	0,17	588
0,70	0,47	0,18	555
0,74	0,54	0,19	526
0,76	0,58	0,20	500
0,78	0,62	0,21	476
0,80	0,65	0,22	454
0,82	0,69	0,23	434
0,84	0,73	0,24	416
0,86	0,76	0,25	400
0,88	0,80	0,26	384
0,90	0,83	0,28	357
0,92	0,87	0,29	344
0,94	0,90	0,30	333
0,96	0,93	0,31	322
0,98	0,97	0,32	312
1,00	1,00	0,33	303
1,02	1,03	0,35	285
1,04	1,07	0.36	277
1,06	1,10	0,38	263
1,08	1,13	0,40	250
1,10	1,16	0,42	238
1,12	1,20	0,43	232
1,14	1,23	0,43	232
1,16	1,26	0,44	227
1,18	1,29	0,46	217
1,20	1,32	0,47	212
1,22	1,35	0,48	208
1,24	1,38	0,51	196
1,26	1,42	0,52	192
1,28	1,45	0,54	185
1,30	1,48	0,56	178
1,32	1,51	0,57	175
1,34	1,54	0,60	166
1,36	1,57	0,62	161
1,38	1,60	0,63	158
1,40	1,63	0,65	153
1,42	1,66	0,68	147
1,44	1,69	0,71	140
1,46	1,72	0,74	135
1,48	1,75	0,78	128
1,50	1,78	0,83	120
1,52	1,81	0,93	107
1,54	1,84	1,04	96
1,56	1,87	1,19	84
1,58	1,89	1,47	68
1,60	1,92	2,22	45
1,62	1,95	5,00	20
1,65	2,00	6,25	16
1,67	2,03	7,69	13
1,70	2,07	10,00	10
1,72	2,10	12,50	8
1,74	2,13	20,00	5
1,76	2,15	25,00	4
1,78	2,18	33,33	3
1,80	2,21	50,00	2
1,82	2,24	100,00	1

IDA CNS / OTU chart based on NOAA

Example

Oxygen partial pressure 1.4 bar.

You now look in the table on the left column and look for the 1.4 bar PO2. These can be found in the right-hand block of the table in the eleventh row. To the right you will find the 1.63, which gives the OTU value per minute at this partial pressure. At the far right of this line, you will find the time in minutes that you can dive with this partial oxygen pressure, namely 153 minutes. These 153 minutes indicate the maximum time you can dive at this oxygen partial pressure during a dive.

If you stay under water at this oxygen partial pressure (1.4 bar) for just 60 minutes, multiply the 1.63 with the dive time in minutes

60 x 1.63 and then you come to the OTU value 97.8

This puts you well below the maximum allowable 700 OTUs per day that IDA recommends.

Therefore, you can, without any problems, make another dive with this partial pressure on the same day. Especially since the surface break has another positive effect on the recovery of the body.

If you now reduce the oxygen partial pressure, you will also get significantly less OTU's per minute.

Example

Gas Mixture Nitrox 34

Oxygen partial pressure on the surface is 0.34 bar.

Diving depth max. 20 meters is equal to 3 bar ambient pressure.

Dive time should be 60 minutes.

0.34 bar PO_2 x 3 bar corresponds to an oxygen partial pressure of 1.02 bar. A look at the table shows an OTU of 1.03. In the right column we can now read the maximum possible dive time of 285 minutes.

For this dive, we now have to count 1.03 times the dive time in minutes, so 60 minutes.

1,03 x 60 is 61,8 OTU

So here are only 61.8 OTU's to be counted.

Based on these calculations, you can see that you can expect to remain submerged for hours on end with a Nitrox mix with 32 or 36% oxygen, without harming your body.

But even if the maximum value of ≤ 700 OTU's per day is barely reached in practice, you should never lose sight of this value for the sake of your health.

Maximum Limit O_2-Exposition											
O_2 – Partial Pressure (bar)	1,6	1,5	1,4	1,3	1,2	1,1	1,0	0,9	0,8	0,7	0,6
Single Exposition (min)	45	120	150	170	210	230	300	350	450	550	710
24 h – Exposition (min)	150	180	180	210	240	270	300	350	450	550	710

From the above table it can be seen at which oxygen partial pressure (O_2 –Partialdruck) you can stay for how long without causing damage to your body.

Example: Oxygen partial pressure 1.4 bar.

A dive can last a maximum of 150 minutes (Einzelexposition). Within 24 hours you can breathe a partial pressure of oxygen of 1.4 bar for a maximum of 180 minutes (24 h Exposition). For example 3 dives to 60 minutes.

Oxygen breathed under increased pressure also has a negative effect on our central nervous system (CNS), which we must also consider. You will also find a value in the table on page 168, more precisely in the third column. This value indicates how much % of the health tolerated dose of hyperbaric oxygen, i.e. oxygen with an increased partial pressure (gas pressure), you can inhale per minute, without causing damage to your central nervous system.

Example

Oxygen partial pressure 1.4 bar

You look again in the left column and look there the 1.4 bar oxygen partial pressure. Then move to the right in the same row until you have landed in the third column with the CNS% / minute.

There you will find the number 0.65. Please remember.

Now you dive and make your dive at an oxygen partial pressure of 1.4 bar and stay under water for 60 minutes. You know that according to the table, that you dive under this pressure, you must multiply the value of 0.65 with every minute. And you know that you should not get over 80% per dive day.

Calculation: 60 minutes x 0.65 = 39 %

Example

Nitrox 32

But now you dive not with an oxygen partial pressure of 1.4 bar but use Nitrox 32, with an oxygen content of 32% and do not go so low that the 1.4 bar oxygen partial pressure will be reached.

Let's assume you go to a maximum depth of 20 meters and stay there for 60 minutes.

With Nitrox 32 you have an oxygen partial pressure of 3 bar x 0.32 bar = 0.96 bar at a depth of 20 meters

So we look at 0.96 bar in the table and find there 0.32 below CNS% / minute.

So now we multiply the 60 minutes with the value 0.32 and then we get 19.2 as a result.

Thus, with this dive, we achieved 19.2% of the maximum oxygen uptake for this dive day.

In theory, we could perform 4 dives of this quality in one day, without fear of damage to the central nervous system.

By maintaining longer surface pauses (SFP), you can also reduce the strain on your CNS.

Reduction factor for surface breaks											
Surface break (min)	0	30	60	90	120	150	180	240	300	360	540
CNS-Faktor	1	0,8	0,63	0,5	0,4	0,31	0,25	0,16	0,1	0,06	0

To do this, take the time of your surface break, say 2 hours (120 minutes), and then look at the factor below, which is 0.4. According to the dive above, you had a CNS load of 19.2% because of the previous dive. Now multiply this 19.2% by 0.4 and then you have 7.68% as a result. Thus, you reduced your CNS load from 19.2% to 7.68% because you had 2 hours surface break. This affects the next dive, since up to 80% of the total oxygen intake per day is allowed. But do not go too far to the limits and take good care of yourself.

Here's a tip for those who do not want to look on tables and calculate everything. Either stay with your Instructor, because these professionals know exactly how long and how deep you can dive without a risk of damage. Or invest in a good dive computer. There, you enter only the 1.4 bar oxygen partial pressure limit, if this is not already done ex works and also type in the oxygen content of your gas mixture. The rest is then taken over by the computer and it also makes sure that nothing happens to you. Provided you always keep an eye on your computer's displays and warnings. If your computer should fail during the dive, you should immediately go to a water depth of 5 meters and stay there for at least 5 minutes before leaving the water. A second dive computer (redundancy) would also be a solution if you want to be completely safe.

Let us now turn to another advantage of Nitrox that is particularly appreciated by those who go diving long and / or often. Among these people are the very ambitious scuba divers as well as instructors, research divers and professional divers.

The keyword is EAD. EAD stands for **equivalent air depth**. If we calculate the EAD before each dive, we can, if necessary, decompress according to the deco table for air (Deko 2000). Then, however, the positive effect of reducing the risk of a decompression accident is lost.

The beauty of Nitrox is that the nitrogen content of our gas mixture is lower than in normal breathing air. Thus, we also absorb less nitrogen and have an advantage in relation to the no-stop time and also during any necessary decompression stops.

If we have less nitrogen in our breathing gas mixture, we reach the "critical" nitrogen partial pressure later than the compressed air diver.

When diving with Nitrox, the EAD is **always** less than the actual depth. Thus, we **always** have a longer no-stop time.

Example

Nitrox 32

32 % Oxygen and 68 % Nitrogen.

Actual diving depth 20 meters, i.e. 3 bar.

Now we have to determine the ratio of nitrogen content to each other, as these significantly influence the decompression.

We call this ratio the Equivalent Factor (EF).

$$EF = \frac{\text{Nitrogen partial pressure } \textbf{Nitrox}}{\text{Nitrogen partial pressure } \textbf{Air}} = \frac{\textbf{0.68}}{\textbf{0.79}} = \textbf{0.86}$$

The EF is 0.86

We now multiply this value by the pressure in the actual diving depth and obtain the equivalent air pressure (EAP).

0.86 x 3 bar = 2.58 bar (EAP)

2.58 bar ambient pressure results in a water depth of 15.8 meters (EAD).

Now let's have a look at the Deko 2000 and see there, in the column up to 18 meters, a no-stop time of 45 minutes. If we had done this dive with compressed air, we would have to use the column up to 21 meters and would have a no-stop time of only 31 minutes.

So by using Nitrox 32 we have a no-stop time that is 14 minutes longer.

Now we take a Nitrox 40 mixture for the same dive. EF calculation as before (take a look at the page before).

EF = 0.76

0.76 x 3 bar = 2.28 bar (EAP)

Now EAD is 12.8 Meter

Thus, we look in the table in the column to 15 meters and get there a no-stop time of 72 minutes.

Compared to pure breathing air, we have a time advantage of 41 minutes.

Whether that is suitable for you or not, you have to decide by yourself. However, you should always, in order not to let it come to accidents, carry a Nitrox suitable dive computer. Nobody stops you from calculating your dives and write notes on your wetnotes Today's dive computers are no longer prone to mistakes, but if it does happen, you'll be prepared if you've thought about it before.

Wetnotes to be fixed

on the forearm.

Made of plastic and rewritable.

Technology and equipment!

In the Nitrox mixture, the oxygen content is, as a rule, significantly higher than in normal breathing air.

Oxygen is an oxidizing gas and it promotes combustion, so does Nitrox.

Nitrox mixtures may only be manufactured by qualified persons using special material (compressors and overflow tanks or membrane systems). Never mix your own gas mixtures if you have not been trained for it before. IDA offers the course Gasblender. The higher the oxygen partial pressure in the mixture, the more violent is the reaction in case of burns or explosions, since oxygen is a strongly oxidizing gas.

In Germany it is regulated by law that a gas mixture containing more than 21% oxygen should be treated like pure oxygen. In other countries, this rule is not so strict.

From these specifications results that our diving equipment

must be **Oxygen suitable**.

Equipment parts are suitable if they have a general oxygen compatibility and are oxygen-clean.

A normal diving equipment must be specially cleaned before use with Nitrox. This process is called "cleaning" in common usage. This cleaning should only be carried out by **specialized personnel**, since all parts of the equipment that come into contact with the increased oxygen content or the pure oxygen must be absolutely clean. After cleaning, the specialist will attach a tank sticker (Nitrox Clean or Oxygen Clean), which confirms the suitability of the diving equipment for Nitrox. The same applies to the regulator and (if we take it strictly) the lifejacket and also the drysuit. So any part that comes directly into contact with the gas and could possibly have oil or grease residues. Before you bring your equipment to "cleaning", make sure that the manufacturer of your equipment has also released them for use with Nitrox. That's not always the case. Some manufacturers of regulators offer corresponding Nitrox regulators "ex works" and also the corresponding diving equipment can be purchased "ex works". Then the first "cleaning" treatment is omitted.

Not compatible with oxygen:

Titanium alloys or titanium, zinc, neoprene, lubricants (oil, grease, silicone)

Oxygen compatible are:

Copper, Teflon, Viton O-rings, special lubricants (Voltalef, Krytox, Fonblin, Tribolub)

Oxygen-clean is our material when it is absolutely clean and free from contamination, especially in the high-pressure area (tank, valve, regulator). Contaminants are oils and greases (exception lubricants, see above), rust particles, soaps and detergents of all kinds.

Tanks, regulators and valves should be inspected once a year by a dealer. This inspection should be confirmed by the dealer with a sticker (Nitrox Clean or Oxygen Clean). The tank should generally be marked with a special sticker or paintwork as a tank for Nitrox so that it will not be accidentally filled at a normal air filling station. The paintwork or the sticker should be large, best around the tank, so it can't not be overlooked.

Example

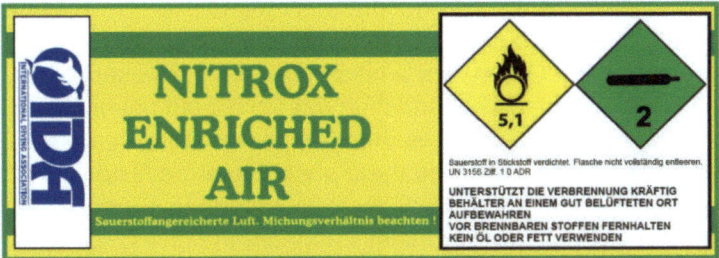

The regulator connection (thread), which is 5/8 inch when using normal breathing air, must be M26 x 2 when using Nitrox to avoid confusion. So a special cylinder valve is needed and the regulator must, after cleaning, also get a special handwheel to the tank connection. However, it is best if you simply get a completely new Nitrox-compatible equipment. That puts you on the safe side.

Note: A filling station for Nitrox offers an oil-free filling, as otherwise explosions may occur. This means that any "non-nitrox-compatible diving tank" can be filled there with normal compressed air. Otherwise, a nitrox tank, which is used exclusively for the use of enriched gases, should never be filled at a normal air filling station, as there no oil-free fillings can be guaranteed. If the tank filled there should later be filled with Nitrox and it is not previously made clean for oxygen use, an explosion can occur. Should it nevertheless happen, the diving equipment must be cleaned again by a specialist before it can be filled with Nitrox.

There are two ways to fill nitrox into a scuba tank. In the so-called partial pressure method, pure oxygen is first filled into the diving tank and then filled up with normal air. Thereafter, the mixture must rest for at least 12 hours to ensure optimal mixing. Working with pure oxygen is very dangerous because oxygen is a very reactive gas and many a compressor shed has lost its roof due to inappropriate handling of pure oxygen. If not worse has happened.

Less dangerous and therefore also "state of the art" in the meantime, is the use of special membrane systems that are able to filter the nitrogen out of the breathing air. With these membrane systems today all common nitrox mixtures can be produced up to an oxygen content of 40%, without the danger of dealing with pure oxygen. The mixture is then ready to use and does not have to rest.

Membrane system

Nitrox is made by filtering out nitrogen.

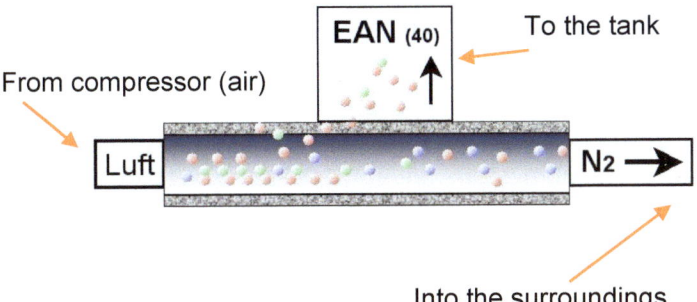

Example photo of a Nitrox filling station

Practice

Before the dive, the following should be noted:

- Is my partner diving with Nitrox? Which mixture does he use and which depth (MOD) can we visit to a maximum?

- If my partner dives with normal air (Nitrox 21 :-), I have to point out to him that I dive with Nitrox and tell him the consequences that result. (Maximum depth, advantages with a possible decompression (EAD), longer bottom times, possible benefits in the case of depth intoxication).

- Gas mixture must be analyzed immediately before the dive and the oxygen content must be noted on the tank label. As an individual and inexpensive tank sticker, it is not meant the nitrox sticker from any of the previous pages, usually a strip of tape is used. The following must be noted on this sticker: percent oxygen percentage, maximum permissible depth with this mixture, name of testing person and date of test. For legal reasons, these data must also be noted in a special filling logbook.

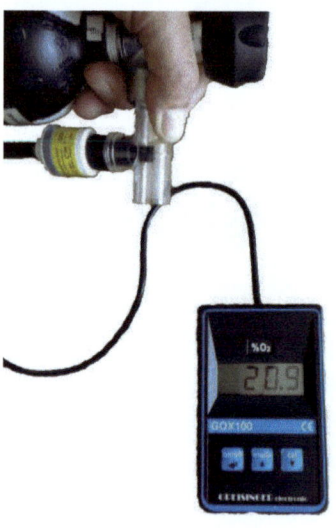

Calibrate the Analyzer with normal

air before checking the Nitrox

mixture of your tank.

(here 20,9 % O_2)

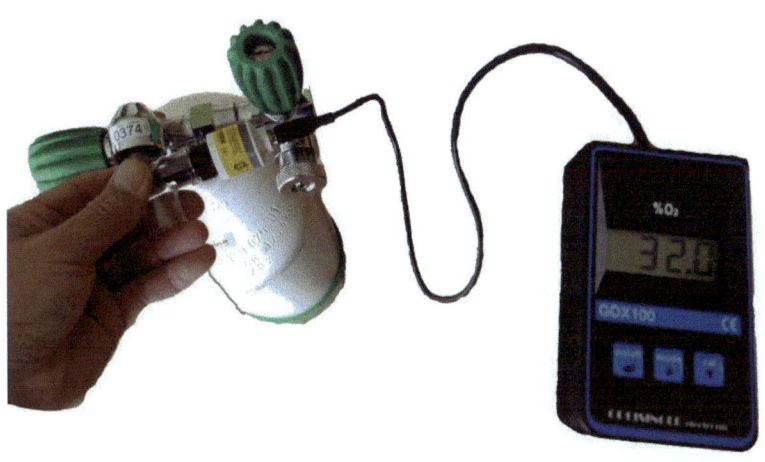

Nitrox 32 perfectly mixed

Than mark the tank

You can do it like this!

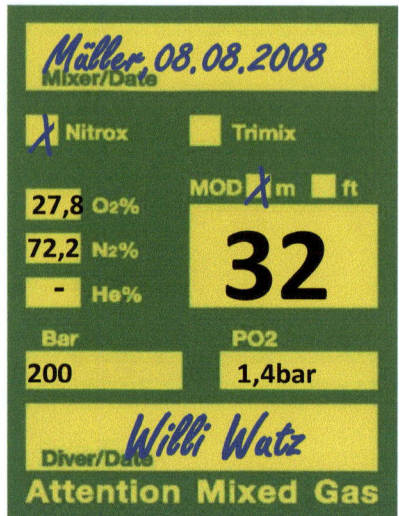

Müller 08.08.2008
Mixer/Date

Nitrox   Trimix

MOD   m   ft

27,8 O2%
72,2 N2%
- He%

32

Bar   PO2
200   1,4bar

Willi Watz
Diver/Date

Attention Mixed Gas

That's better! ☺

- The dive computer must be set to the correct mixture.

- The dive computer must be set to the maximum oxygen partial pressure of 1.4 bar. Often this setting is already adjusted ex works.

During the dive, the following should be noted:

- MOD (max. diving depth) must not be exceeded.

- Control of the partner for possible oxygen intolerance, if he/she dives with Nitrox.

- Self-check for possible oxygen intolerance.

- If your instructor has placed a safety deco tank at a depth of 5 meters in order to allow the divers who run out of air the safety decompression stop, pay attention to the contents of this tank. The breathing gas in this tank should always have the same composition as the breathing gas you use. If this diving tank has a content of more oxygen than your own diving equipment, this is relatively uncritical, since this does not affect the subsequent dives and if anything, then only positive, in terms of decompression. The additional oxygen effect (OTU / CNS) is negligible at a deco stop of a few minutes. However, if there is a gas mixture in this decompression tank which has a lower oxygen content than your own breathing gas mixture, this is not uncritical. Because your dive computer calculates for this dive and also for possible repetitive dives with the previously entered values, so for example with Nitrox 36. However, perhaps is Nitrox 21, which is compressed air, in the safety deco tank, which can have a negative effect on your residual nitrogen saturation in the body, since you are not breathing 64% nitrogen (Nitrox 36) but 79% nitrogen (compressed air). Many dive computers have the ability to set a second breathing gas and then consider that gas for decompression and subsequent dives. If you perform such dives frequently, with safety stops on 5 meters, you buy such a dive computer and learn to handle it properly and make the correct settings.

After the dive, the following should be noted:

- Write the dive with all information in your logbook.

- Write the residual pressure of the tank on the control sheet and the tank sticker (e.g. tape).

- The person refilling the diving tank must attach a new sticker with the corresponding data. Percent of oxygen percentage, maximum permissible depth with this mixture, name of the examiner and the date of the test.

Always follow the guidelines and laws that apply in the country in which you dive. There are for example, countries in which a freshly mixed nitrox mixture may be used for a maximum of 30 days or countries in which the color coding of the diving tanks is different. If you are unsure, ask your base leader or your instructor.

If you dive with Nitrox frequently, even at home, you should get your own analyzer. Then you can ensure that you always have exactly the mixture in your scuba, which should be in it. Observe the specifications of the manufacturer and bear in mind that the oxygen sensor also has to be replaced from time to time (with modern devices, the sensor will last about 2 to 3 years). Always keep in mind that the correct amount of oxygen in your breathing gas mixture is very important because your life depends on it. If possible, check your gas mixture more than once and, if possible, do not let your diving equipment out of sight after checking it.

Keep a record of your nitrox dives so you and the others can comprehend what happened to you in the event of an accident and why the accident might have happened.

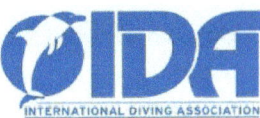

IDA Nitroxplaner

Name, first name:	
Date, time:	
Place	
Diving site:	
Name, first name of the partner	
Name, first name of the partner	

Planning data		
CNS O_2 % before the dive	CNS O_2 %	
Repetitive group and surface break	RG:	SB
Gas mixture (EAN % O_2)	fO_2 :	fN_2 :
O_2 – Proportion measured	O_2 % :	Date
Gas in stock barL = P x V (Note the reserve)		
O_2- partial pressure(max. 1,4 bar) $pPO_2 = fO_2 \times P$		
Max. depth (MOD in m) $MOP = pPO_2 / fO_2$		

Dive planning		Analysis
	Planned	Carried out
Depth and ambient pressure		
Equivalent depht (EAD) $EAP = PpN_2 / 0,79$ bar		
Bottom time		
Dekoplan (Deko 2000 ____ over sea level		
Safety stop 3 min. / 5 meter		
Total diving time		
Gas consuption (barl)		
CNS O_2 % - Total (IDA CNS table)		
CNS O_2 % - Increase		
Signature		

Many dive centers that offer EAN gas mixtures also carry a so-called fill log, which contains special data pertaining to the filled diving tank. Therefore, if you pick up a freshly filled diving tank there, with the gas mixture corresponding to your diving depth, you often have to acknowledge receipt. This signature is primarily for the safety of the person who has filled your diving tank and secondarily for your own safety. Since on the control sheet also the serial number or an inventory number of the diving tank, given by the diving base, is written. This is to prevent accidental interchange of the diving tank. Check both this number and the contents of the diving tank (gas analysis) before signing the filling sheet. On the following page you will find an IDA fill sheet design.

Nitrox Filling logbook

I, _____, hereby certify

First name, name

that I have the diving tank with the number: _____

Serial or inventory number of the tank

on _____ subjected to a gas analysis.

date

I received the tank on _____ from

date

_____

Name of the diving base / the instructor

and measured an oxygen content of _____ %

The gas mixture was made by _____

Name of the gasblender

and labeled as_____

Oxygen content (e.g. Nitrox 32)

This means that I can dive with this breathing gas mixture to a

maximum depth of _____meter.

The filling pressure of the tank is_____ bar.

_____   _____

First name and name of the diver   Signature of the diver

So, that was it for now. Now you can get started and gain experience. Take care of yourself and have the courage to even break off a dive or not even go into the water, if you do not feel well. A good diving partner understands this. Safety is the most important thing. And keep in mind, a good diving partner is the best life insurance you can have but

"No buddy is perfect"

and so even your diving partner can make mistakes. So take care of yourself and have a lot of fantastic dives.

Note of thanks!

Hereby I would like to thank the following friends for having read my treatise several times, so that I can be sure that I have not told nonsense to you. I especially thank my darling Karen for accepting my intuitive punctuation and guiding her into appropriate paths. The comma has always been my friend, or alternatively my enemy. ☺ My problem is that the English punctuation does not match the German one at all. I'm very sorry, please excuse it. I'm a diving instructor and a Radar electronics technician not a grammar teacher.

Karen Fink

Thomas Freudenberg, chairman of the Instructor Examination board of IDA, Master Chief Officer and Diving Instructor of the German Navy, Professional Diver and member of the German Industry and commerce chamber for professional divers.

Thomas Burkhardt, former chief of the IDA Instructor Examination board.

What is IDA - International Diving Association?

IDA is an international association of diving instructors and member of CMAS Germany and R.S.T.C. (Recreational Scuba Training Council). IDA trains divers and diving instructors worldwide.

Scuba is the shortcut for „**S**elf **C**ontained **U**nderwater **B**reathing **A**pparatus"!

IDA was founded in 1996 and since then has been very successful in trying to reconcile the American "Easy Diving" with the "European (German) will to perfection". This does not always work 100%. Nonetheless, IDA has managed to license nearly 1600 IDA Instructors around the world who are training and checking divers under the IDA guidelines. IDA is a partner of CMAS Germany and a member of R.S.T.C. Both organizations cover about 90% of the international diving education market with their member associations and ensure that you can safely learn and enjoy diving for years to come.

7. Appendix

Here is an excerpt from the recommendation for the dive group compilation of the IDA:

Only the allowed pairings are mentioned.

Open Water Diver or Diver *

and

Advanced Open Water Diver	to 18 meter depth
Diver**	to 20 meter depth
Master Scuba Diver	to 20 meter depth
from Diver *** and higher	to 40 meter depth

Junior Open Water Diver

and

Diveguide and / or higher (Assistant Instructor or Instructor) to 8 meter depth.

Generally, according to IDA recommendation and age, the following maximum depths apply:

8 – 10 years	**5 meter**
10 – 12 years	**5 meter**
12 – 16 years	**12 meter**
16 – 18 years	**25 meter**
From 18 years	**40 meter**

Glossary:

50 bar rule

50 bar residual pressure is the safety reserve and should not be part of the diving calculation

40m

Depth limit for Recreational diver

No-stop-time dives

IDA recommend no-stop-time dives

Descent speed / rate

Max. 30 m / min.

Safety stop

3 minutes at 5 meters at every dive which leads deeper than 5 meters

Surface pause

IDA recommend a surface pause of at least 2 hours between two dives

Repetitive dives

IDA recommend to make not more than two dives a day

Order

IDA recommend to make the deepest dive at first

Compression phase

Pressure increase during descent

Isopression phase

Constant pressure, the diver remains at a constant depth

Variopression phase

Changing ambient pressure corresponds to the real one

dive profile

Decompression phase

Pressure decrease on ascent

No-stop-time

The time you can stay in a certain depth of water

in which a decompression stop is not necessary

Bottom time

The time from the descent to the beginning of the ascent

Ascent time

The time, without decompression pauses, which is needed for the pure ascent

BMV Breath minute volume

The amount of air you need to breathe in a minute, at the surface

Decompression stop

Length of stay at a certain depth level to give the nitrogen the chance to leave the body.

Surface pause

The time between two dives

No Fly Time

The time which should lie between the last dive and a flight, since in the aircraft cabin a reduced air pressure prevails. This reduced cabin pressure can lead in extreme cases to a decompression sickness. This time should, for safety's sake, always be more than 24 hours.

Instructor

Shortcut for diving instructor.

Assistant Instructor

Shortcut for the Assistant of the diving instructor.

Wet recompression

to bring the injured diver back to pressure by diving again.

Share air

Spending air to the partner by using the own regulator

Please read all points carefully before signing the form and respond truthfully. Diving is a sport that requires some fitness and good health. The correct answer to these questions is necessary so that your Instructor can see if you are fit for diving. With your signature, you release all employees and also the base or dive school operator (s) from any liability with regard to your state of health. Please note that the IDA recommends that you consult a doctor before the first dive, who will examine your suitability for diving. This form only serves to enable you to dive if you are healthy and no qualified doctor is available. If your health changes during the diving course or during the dives, you are obliged to inform the dive center management immediately. You may only dive if you are healthy or, for example in diabetes, are well adjusted. Persons suffering from heart disease or having severe colds should not dive as well as persons under the influence of drugs, alcohol or other drugs. Even people with extreme overweight or underweight are not suitable for scuba diving unless the doctor decides otherwise. Since diving errors or the handling of the diving equipment can have serious health consequences, you are obliged to dive exclusively under the guidance of a qualified instructor, instructor assistant or dive guide. If you need explanations about the questions below, please contact your instructor before answering the question.

Please answer the following questions in writing with a yes or a no. Your instructor will decide if he will let you dive. If you answer yes to any of these questions, you should consult a doctor before diving.

Medical questionnaire for divers

For the participant:

The following questions should clarify whether you should be examined by a doctor before diving. If you answer one of the questions with a "yes", that does not mean that you are not allowed to dive, but your instructor then decides if you can dive or being send to a doctor for examination. If in doubt, you should consult a doctor. Please take your time answering the questions below.

Do you have or did you had....

Asthma, difficulty breathing or breathing problems during exercise..

Hay fever or bouts of allergies
....

Common colds, sinus problems or bronchitis
....

A lung disease (e.g. pneumothorax).......................................

A lung tear ....

Diseases or operations in the thorax
....

Wear a pacemaker ....

You suffer from mental problems (panic anxiety, fear of

tight spaces)..

You suffer from neurological problems ....

Suffering from a chronic illness ....

You suffer from epilepsy or other seizure disorders ....

You suffer from migraine headaches ....

Have you ever lost consciousness ....

You suffer greatly from motion sickness (car or boat)..................

You suffer from severe diarrhea or dehydration ....

Have you ever had a diving accident (e.g. decompression sickness)..

Do you have problems with physical activity?.............................

Have you had a head injury with unconsciousness in the last 6 years? ....

You suffer from recurrent back problems...................................

Are you (possibly) pregnant ....

Take medications (except malaria prophylaxis and "Pill")............

Are you a smoker..

Are you in medical care ....

Suffering from elevated cholesterol ....

Have you ever had a heart attack or stroke? ....

Had one of your family members ever had a heart attack or stroke ....

You suffer from diabetes ....

Did you have a surgical procedure on the spine or back? ....

Do you have problems due to surgery on the arms or legs? ....

You suffer from blood pressure disorders or take medication against it ....

Suffer from a blood clot (thrombosis)..

Do you suffer from heart disease (angina pectoris or similar)........

Have you ever undergone a surgical procedure on the heart or on a blood vessel? ....

Suffer from dizziness or temporary hearing loss ....

Have you ever been operated on the sinuses? ....

Have you ever been operated on the ears? ....

Do you have problems with the ears ....

Do you have an artificial bowel outlet ....

Take sporty supplements ....

Have you ever been treated for drug addiction (including alcohol)? ....

Have you ever had a soft-tissue fracture (hernias)............................

Do you have problems with the blood ....

Have you undergone surgery within the last 6 weeks ....

Do you have an acute stomach ulcer ....

Do you have problems with pressure equalization? ....

Do you have fever ....

If you currently suffer from the following conditions or illnesses you are not suitable for diving. This also applies if these conditions or illnesses occur during the diving course or vacation.

Pressure equalization problems

Colds, inflammation of the sinuses

Any kind of breathing problems (bronchitis, hay fever)

stomach ulcers

Influence of drugs of any kind (including alcohol)

Pregnancy

Fever

Dizziness

Nausea, seasickness

Diarrhea, dehydration

Migraine or severe headache

Surgical intervention of any kind made within the last 6 weeks

I have the above list today ....

carefully read, understood and noted. So I'm sure I'm fit for diving. My instructor told me that if I had to answer "yes" to any of the questions above, I should consult a doctor or seek medical advice. I declare that I have answered the questionnaire truthfully.

Name, first name:...

Address:..

Date of birth, place of birth:..

Signature:...

Signature of the parent / guardian at minors:...........................

Questions and Answers Nitrox Diver *

1. What is the maximum variation (+/-) allowed in O2 analysis?

a 3 %

b 5 %

c 1 %

d 2 %

2. What mixtures are you allowed to use as an IDA Nitrox * diver?

a EAN 28, EAN 32, EAN 50

b EAN 28 and EAN 34

c EAN 32 and EAN 36

d mixtures between 21 % to 40 % O2

3. What is the maximum partial oxygen pressure for IDA Nitrox * divers?

a 1,6 bar

b 1,4 bar

c 1,2 bar

d 1,0 bar

4. Use the formula (T in the circle) to calculate the MOD for EAN 34.

a 37 m

b 33 m

c 31 m

d 25 m

5. Use the formula (T in the circle) to determine the exact partial pressure of oxygen at 21.0 m with EAN 28.

a 0,87 bar

b 0,59 bar

c 1,12 bar

d 0,62 bar

6. What should be considered with regard to diving equipment used with more than 40 % O2?

7. Explain the Paul Bert effect and name at least 3 medical symptoms.

8. Explain the following terms: MOD – EAN 32 – EAD - CNS O2?

9. Which characteristic data of breathing gas mixture must be noted on an adhesive label on the diving tank?

10. Why is handling oxygen so dangerous?

11. Name at least 4 advantages of Nitrox.

12. What does „oxygen compatible" mean?

Solutions Nitrox Diver *

Question	A	B	C	D
1			■	
2				■
3		■		
4			■	
5	■			

To 6

The equipment must be suitable for Nitrox. i. e. oxygen clean.

To 7

The „Paul Bert" effect describes the poisoning of the central nervous system (CNS) by oxygen.

Muscle tremors, twitching and convulsions, eye disturbances, visual disturbances, malaise, nausea, sensory disturbances, confusion, metallic taste, inner ear disturbances (dizziness), ringing in the ear.

To 8

MOD = Maximum Operating Depth

EAN 32 = Enriched Air Nitrox 32 % O2 – Nitrox 32 % O2

EAD = Equivalent Air Depth

CNS O2 % = Central Nervous System Oxygen %

To 9

Mixture e. g. EAN 32

Content e. g. 31,8 % O2

MOD e. g. 34 m

Date e. g. 07.12.2022

Bottler e. g. Karsten

To 10

Oxygen promotes combustion

To 11

Less nitrogen uptake

Reduced risk of depth intoxication

Less risk of DCS, when using air tables

Less nitrogen bubbles (micro bubbles)

Less fatigue after diving

To 12

Materials that do not react with oxygen e. g. brass, stainless steel, Viton (O-rings)

Notes:

Notes: